ALAN SPENCE is an award-winning poet and playwright, novelist and short story writer. In 1996 he won the McVitie's Prize for Scottish Writer of the Year. He is based in Edinburgh where he and his wife run the Sri Chinmoy Meditation Centre. He is Professor in Creative Writing at the University of Aberdeen, where he is also Artistic Director of the annual WORD Festival.

also by Alan Spence

ALAN SPENCE

CLEAR LIGHT

HAIKU

CANONGATE

Edinburgh · New York · Melbourne

First published in Great Britain in 2005 by
Canongate Books Ltd,
14 High Street Edinburgh EH1 1TE

10 9 8 7 6 5 4 3 2 1

 Scottish **Arts** Council

The publishers gratefully
acknowledge subsidy from the
Scottish Arts Council towards
the publication of this volume

British Library Cataloguing-in-Publication Data
A catalogue record for this book is available on
request from the British Library

ISBN 1 84195 664 3

Typeset in Adobe Garamond by Forge Design
Printed and bound by WS Bookwell, Finland

www.canongate.net

To Janani

ACKNOWLEDGEMENTS

Some of these poems have appeared in the following:

Chapman, Goldfish Suppers (Edinburgh Council), *Island, Northern Writes* (Aberdeenshire Council), *Panorama, Poetry Scotland, Sampark* (India), *Scottish Poetry Library Website, Still* (Ingleby Gallery) and on a card produced by the University of Aberdeen.

as if I've never
seen it before –
the new moon

spring snow
trying its best
not to fall

all morning the drip
of melting snow
from the trees

the dark chapel
white rose a chalice
of light

suddenly spring –
my heart and the river
full to bursting

that daft dog
chasing the train
then letting it go

the washing
hung out to dry –
the spring rain

in the drizzling rain
blaze of yellow
blossoms

the rain has stopped
but still it's falling
under the trees

under the vast sky
the horse rolls over
kicks his legs in the air

plovers on the wet sand
each one standing
on its own reflection

black crow stark
against the field
of yellow rape

white butterfly –
the sun in my eyes
makes me sneeze

I'm falling up
into it –
big summer sky

mountain-tops
in the clear blue
above the clouds

borobodur
the buddha's lives
dreamed in stone

borobodur
rumble of thunder
the buddha's gaze

borobodur
what the thunder said
borobodur

high summer –
strawberry birthmark
on the old man's face

no change
for the beggar –
the heat beats down

honeysuckle? jasmine?
the faintest trace
in the night air

above the trees
above the clouds –
distant volcano

acrid summer smell –
old dust damped down
by sudden rain

drift of incense
shimmer of sitar music
long ago

summer rainstorm
the afternoon raga
quickening

all night long
that single
mosquito

the toy windmill
glints as it spins –
summer breeze

summer haircut –
the cool breeze
on my neck

big bruised clouds –
the colour
of the storm

two-day headache –
I'll blame it
on the weather

unbearable heat —
the sudden rush of rain
brings ease

soothing me asleep
the hush
of the rain

4 a.m.
shaken awake
by the thunder

morning glories
wide open
to the rain

summer downpour
can't rain any harder
but it does

summer downpour –
even the carp take shelter
under the bridge

monsoon rains —
the carp, openmouthed
leap out of the pond

tropical rainstorm
five days
straight

am I really here?
sunset over the
south china sea

the sun plunges
into the ocean
the ocean overflows

summer thunderstorm
zigzag of lightning
cracks the sky

after the lightning
holding our breath
till the thunder

morning after the storm —
sun raising steam
from the fields

after the rains
breathing deep the scent
of eucalyptus

tiny starflowers
bright yellow
among the green

the ruined temple
torn apart / held together
by the roots of trees

the ruined temple –
tree-roots have cracked open
the buddha's head

indonesian rain –
the gamelan builds
its measured frenzy

bright morning
that bird I can't name
singing singing singing

the drunk rolling home
the early morning jogger –
a grin and a wave

baby duck so light
it *runs* across the leaves
of the waterlily

dapple of light
on the page
making this poem

paper birds –
their shadows
flying

deeper into the forest
and deeper still –
the silence

they spark a moment
fireflies
then the deeper dark

dumb bumblebee
bumps the windowpane
again again again

a world away
from home –
sharp scent of broom

dawn light –
old man fishing
the wide silver river

husk of a cicada
empty
of its cry

almost autumn –
sunflower, head bent
in the rain

borrowed landscape –
the distant hills
framed in my window

the setting sun
turns every window
to stained glass

only
the wind in the trees
the far blue hills

the late bee
drowned in a jar
of honey

boats at anchor
cables clanking –
musselburgh gamelan

wind-chimes
the only sound
in the meditation room

bright autumn day —
a red yacht
with purple sails!

every autumn
that has ever been –
the tree half green half gold

leaf on the river
this moment
here now

quiet place
by the river –
a good day for haiku

pure blue of sea
and sky this clear
september day

autumn contentment —
watching the river,
listening to the crows

autumn shower –
taking shelter
in a tea-shop

two hawks
moving not moving
in the high air

the light fades
the mountain turns
a deeper blue

kamakura buddha –
my back straightens
of itself

midnight, my shadow
thrown on the wall –
the full moon

late evening light
just touching
the tops of the trees

the child's red kite
surging, surging
against the wind

yellow chrysanthemum
holding the last light
of the day

the oystercatcher's cry —
cold loneliness,
the far north

as if
any of it mattered –
the autumn wind

pure emptiness –
low tide
the waning moon

it's just the wind
in my eyes, she says,
explaining the tears

between the road
and the railway line –
abandoned boat

old burnt-out car
rusting away
in the autumn field

autumn dusk
the musty smell
of an old book

secondhand bookshop –
my own books
musty as the rest

cloud of starlings
turning as one
in the evening light

shining half-moon –
a white cat slips out
from the shadows

sleeping alone –
all night that gate
banging in the wind

autumn night
the unanswered phone
in the next room

autumn night
the moon's a paper lantern
hung in the sky

flying his kite –
a sudden gust lifts him
off his feet

after the storm
the smell of the sea
miles inland

turning back the clocks –
how dark the night
how cold

halloween –
the day darkens
three cows form a coven

grey rainy day
in the park a solitary
blue umbrella

making tea
as if nothing
had happened

walking
at the slow pace
of his old dog

bonfire night storm
the fireworks drowned out
by the thunder

overheated
the latenight train
far from home

the small hours
the seagull's cry
asking who I am

my father's face
looking back at me
from the mirror

november afternoon
even the wind
is grey

pre-dawn cold
the clang of a bell
in the convent

breathe in
this moment
breathe out

cold light
the sea and sky
ice blue

the red path
across the water
to the rising sun

winter morning –
running in the clouds
of my breath

without thinking
saying good morning
to the mountain

mountain in mist
single brushstroke
on a blank page

after everything
the simple absolution
of the rain

winter afternoon –
the cold has drained all colour
from the day

winter afternoon
full moon shining
mother-of-pearl sky

the early dark –
an empty wheelchair
outside the pub

short cold dark day –
shop empty, the barber
cuts his own hair

dark afternoon
sitting here watching
an old *film noir*

cold dank saturday –
stale jumblesale smell
of the charity shop

blue neon
shining up at me
from the wet pavement

rain at night –
in the end
it comes to this

just the cold
just the rain
just the night

chant from the mosque —
there is one god, allah ...
cold aberdeen night

the cold rain
relentless neverending
across rannoch moor

with every gust
the winter rain
stinging harder

this cold winter night –
the sticky floor
of the chinese takeaway

grey scottish day –
the japanese girl smiles,
gives me this poem

even so, even so ...
reading issa,
the end of the year

rain falling
through the night
into the new year

piecing together
the metal flute –
so cold

the cold flute
warming up
as I play

the day passes
rain becomes sleet
becomes snow

the rubbish in the street
is also graced
by this fall of snow

winter swingpark –
the plastic horse
riderless

cold dark night
baby boy crying –
his first winter

shaving cut
stinging this cold
winter morning

the snow turns to slush,
freezes over –
the short winter day

solitary figure
crossing the vast
expanse of snow

the seagull turning
grey
against the snow

the burnt-out apartment
charred furniture outside
in the snow

midwinter night
mind clear and cold
moonlight on snow

solitude –
snow falling endlessly
into itself

the silver world —
glitter of snow
in the moonlight

shrieks in the cold air –
a snowball fight
in the graveyard

one small dog –
two hundred geese
panicked into flight

does that dog
have the buddha-nature?
hear him bark!

scattering
her father's ashes
as the snow falls

the storm has passed
the mountains are mountains
everything clear

clear cold night –
through the tree's bare branches
the stars

this bright morning
glass buddha
in the clear light